KWANZAA

by Dr. Artika R. Tyner

PEBBLE
a capstone imprint

Published by Pebble, an imprint of Capstone.
1710 Roe Crest Drive
North Mankato, Minnesota 56003
capstonepub.com

Library of Congress Cataloging-in-Publication Data
Names: Tyner, Artika R., author.
Title: Kwanzaa / Dr. Artika R. Tyner.
Description: North Mankato, Minnesota : Pebble Explore, An Imprint of Capstone, [2022] | Series: Traditions and celebrations | Includes bibliographical references and index. | Audience: Ages 5-8 | Audience: Grades K-1 | Summary: "Kwanzaa is about celebrating! It honors African American heritage. Some people mark the holiday by lighting the kinara. Families and friends gather to eat a big feast. Readers will discover how a shared holiday can have multiple traditions and be celebrated in all sorts of ways" —Provided by publisher.
Identifiers: LCCN 2021012671 (print) | LCCN 2021012672 (ebook) | ISBN 9781663908438 (hardcover) | ISBN 9781663920942 (paperback) | ISBN 9781663908407 (ebook pdf) | ISBN 9781663908421 (kindle edition)
Subjects: LCSH: Kwanzaa—Juvenile literature. | African Americans—Social life and customs—Juvenile literature. | Holidays—Juvenile literature.
Classification: LCC GT4403 .T96 2022 (print) | LCC GT4403 (ebook) | DDC 394.2612—dc23
LC record available at https://lccn.loc.gov/2021012671
LC ebook record available at https://lccn.loc.gov/2021012672

Image Credits
Alamy: Cultura Creative RF, 13, Jonathan ORourke, 9; Getty Images: S847, 24; Newscom: MCT/John VanBeekum, 26, MCT/Trish Tyson, 1, UPI Photo Service/ Bill Greenblatt, 21, ZUMA Press/Boyzell Hosey, 11, 19, 22, ZUMA Press/Bruce R. Bennett, 23, ZUMA Press/Owen Brewer, 17, Science Source/Lawrence Migdale, 14, 25; Shutterstock: Ailisa, Cover, Cat Act Art, 7, Kasabutskaya Nataliya, 6; SuperStock/Kwame Zikomo, 5, 29

Artistic elements: Shutterstock: Rafal Kulik

Editorial Credits
Editor: Erika L. Shores; Designer: Dina Her; Media Researcher: Jo Miller; Production Specialist: Tori Abraham

All internet sites appearing in back matter were available and accurate when this book was sent to press.

TABLE OF CONTENTS

Words in **bold** are in the glossary.

WHAT IS KWANZAA?

Kendra lights a black candle. It is the first day of Kwanzaa. Kendra's father will read them a book about Marcus Garvey. He was a leader who helped bring together African people around the world.

Kwanzaa **celebrates** African **culture**. African Americans learn about Africa and their **heritage**. The holiday starts on December 26 and ends on January 1.

WHAT KWANZAA MEANS

Kwanzaa means "first" in the East African language of Swahili. It is a celebration of the first fruit of the harvest. This is when people gather crops from the land. Some of the crops are cassava, yams, and beans. Cassava is a root vegetable used in many African dishes.

beans

cassava

African harvest festivals are a **tradition**. Sometimes the weather was bad and crops did not grow. Other times African farmers grew plenty of food. They would celebrate the harvest with food, family, and friends.

HISTORY OF KWANZAA

Dr. Maulana Karenga started the Kwanzaa holiday in 1966. He wanted to bring the African American community together. It is a special time for African Americans to learn about their history.

Kwanzaa lasts seven days. The goal is to remember the meaning of community and where you come from. People celebrate and learn community **values**.

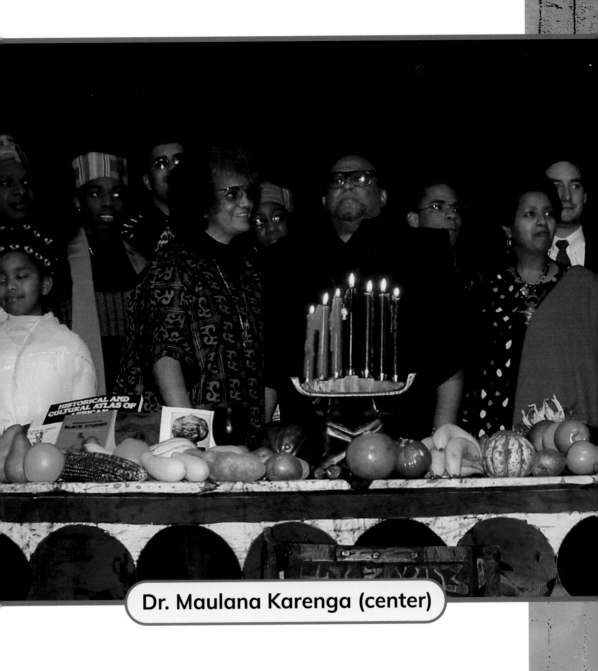

Dr. Maulana Karenga (center)

Each day, grown-ups teach children about a community value:

- Umoja (unity) means coming together as one people.

- Kujichagulia (self-determination) means to be responsible for yourself.

- Ujima (collective responsibility) means working together.

- Ujamaa (cooperative economics) means **supporting** local Black businesses.

- Nia (purpose) means remembering African and African American history.

- Kuumba (creativity) means to work to make the community beautiful.

- Imani (faith) means hope for the future.

On the first day of Kwanzaa, people talk about why unity (umoja) matters. A black candle is lit. On each of the next six days, a new value is taught. Another candle is lit.

People prepare for Kwanzaa by setting a special table. The kinara is placed on the table. The kinara holds seven candles. A black candle is in the middle. It is surrounded by three green and three red candles.

The black candle stands for African people everywhere. Green candles are the land and hope for the future. Red candles are for those who came before us. Each night of Kwanzaa, households light a candle together.

The kinara is placed on a woven mat. The mat is called a mkeka. It shows how the past connects to the present.

In honor of the harvest, a bowl of fruits and vegetables is placed on the table. Ears of corn are put on the table too. Each ear of corn stands for children. They are hope for the future. The unity cup is a way to show that a family stands together as one.

Children decorate their homes. They hang African art and crafts on the walls. People might bring out their favorite musical instruments. These include the djembe (drum), kalimba (thumb piano), and caxixi (shaker).

KWANZAA AT SCHOOL

Many students learn about holiday celebrations at school. Children explore the cultures of the world. Learning about Kwanzaa connects children to the **continent** of Africa.

Children can learn about Kwanzaa at school through:

- Reading stories about African history and culture

- Listening to a community member speak about African culture

- Drawing or crafting a kinara or a mkeka

- Watching a video about Kwanzaa

- Learning words in Swahili

CELEBRATING KWANZAA AROUND THE WORLD

Kwanzaa is an important way for African Americans to connect with their African roots. Many African Americans are from West Africa. The **enslavement** of Africans by Europeans and Americans began here.

Children study maps, books, and videos. They find out about the 54 countries in Africa. They learn more about African history. They learn about where Black people came from, and the languages, traditions, and values of Africans.

Children are taught new words in Swahili to celebrate Kwanzaa. The word *harambee* means "let's pull together." This is about bringing the community together.

Kwanzaa is celebrated by Black people around the world. There are more than 1 billion people with African roots. Kwanzaa is a way to connect African people from many countries.

People mark the holiday of Kwanzaa through service. This means they help those in need. This is ujima in action.

Local groups and communities come together to celebrate Kwanzaa. Some hold events at a park or library in their neighborhoods. Others create community plays or hold African drumming events.

People practice ujamaa by supporting local Black businesses. They buy shea butter, jewelry, black soap, and other things from shops owned by Black artists. Black soap is made from plants. Some people say it has health benefits.

black soap

People might dress in beautiful kente cloth. Kente is a colorful woven fabric from the country of Ghana. Women wear long beautiful dresses. Men wear **dashikis** and a **kufi** hat. Children also dress up for this special celebration.

Kwanzaa ends with a big celebration. People share gifts called zawadis. A zawadi may be a framed family photo or a new Black history book.

It is a time to feast with loved ones. West African dishes like **jollof** and groundnut stew are cooked. People also enjoy **soul food** dishes, such as collard greens and candied yams. Soul food comes from African American southern cooking.

Remember Kendra celebrating Kwanzaa? Her family invites her grandparents to their home. They gather for the last day of Kwanzaa and enjoy a big meal.

Kendra's father plays the djembe drum. The family enjoys a soul food feast. Kendra opens her zawadi and finds a beautiful book about Africa.

GLOSSARY

celebrate (SE-luh-brayt)—to do something special for an event or holiday

continent (KAHN-tuh-nuhnt)—one of earth's seven large land masses

culture (KUHL-chuhr)—a people's way of life, ideas, art, customs, and traditions

dashiki (da-SHEE-kee)—a loose, brightly colored shirt that first came from West Africa

enslavement (in-SLAYV-muhnt)—the act of making someone lose their freedom

heritage (HER-uh-tij)—history and traditions handed down from the past

jollof (JOW-luhf)—a rice dish popular in West Africa

kufi (koo-FEE)—a close-fitting round hat without a brim

soul food (SOHL FOOD)—traditional food eaten by southern African Americans

support (suh-PORT)—to help or encourage someone

tradition (truh-DISH-uhn)—a custom, idea, or belief passed down through time

value (VAL-yoo)—a belief or idea that is important to a person or group

READ MORE

Erlic, Lily. *Kwanzaa*. New York: Smartbook Media Inc., 2021.

Linde, Barbara M. *Celebrating Kwanzaa*. New York: Gareth Stevens Publishing, 2020.

Shofner, Melissa Raé. *Story Behind Kwanzaa*. New York: PowerKids Press, 2020.

INTERNET SITES

Kwanzaa
cbc.ca/kidscbc2/the-feed/all-about-kwanzaa

Kwanzaa
pbskids.org/arthur/holidays/kwanzaa/

Kwanzaa
kids.nationalgeographic.com/celebrations/article/kwanzaa

INDEX

HOW TO SAY IT

caxixi (CA-shee-shee)

djembe (JEM-bay)

harambee (her-AAM-bee)

imani (ee-MAH-nee)

kalimba (kuh-LIM-buh)

kente (KEN-tay)

kinara (ki-NAH-rah)

kujichagulia (koo-jee-cha-goo-LEE-ah)

kuumba (koo-OOM-bah)

mkeka (em-KEH-kah)

nia (NEE-ah)

ujamaa (oo-JAH-mah)

ujima (oo-JEE-mah)

umoja (oo-MOH-jah)

zawadi (ZA-wah-dee)